Text, Don't Call

An Illustrated Guide to
the Introverted Life

INFJoe

A TarcherPerigee Book

tarcherperigee

An imprint of Penguin Random House LLC
375 Hudson Street
New York, New York 10014

LIBRARY OF CONGRESS CATALOGING-IN-PUBLICATION DATA
Names: Caycedo-Kimura, Aaron T., author.
Title: Text, don't call : an illustrated guide to the introverted life /
   Aaron T. Caycedo-Kimura.
Description: New York, NY : TarcherPerigee, [2017] |
Identifiers: LCCN 2017004484 (print) | LCCN 2017016215 (ebook)
   | ISBN 9781524704599 | ISBN 9780143130789
Subjects: LCSH: Introversion. | Introverts.
Classification: LCC BF698.35.I59 (ebook) | LCC BF698.35.I59 C39 2017
(print)
   | DDC 155.2/32—dc23
LC record available at https://lccn.loc.gov/2017004484

Printed in the United States of America
10 9 8 7 6 5 4 3 2 1

Book design by Sabrina Bowers

To my wife, Luisa,
to the memory of my parents,
and to introverts everywhere

Yeah, Honey, another book about introverts. I just don't get it.
Well, this one has pictures!

Contents

Introduction

Have you ever wondered why you don't enjoy parties? Or why you need so much time to yourself? Do you sometimes feel like an outsider, even with your closest friends? Do you often feel that you're running on empty? If your answer is a resounding yes to these questions, you're not weird, and you're certainly not alone. You just may be an introvert.

In 1997, while my fiancée (now wife) and I were soul-searching for what to do with our lives, we came across the book *Do What You Are* by Paul D. Tieger and Barbara Barron, which walked us through personality typing based on the Myers-Briggs Type Indicator (MBTI) inventory. The MBTI tool is an assessment designed to measure a person's psychological preferences of perception and judgment, determined by where the person falls on the continua of four dichotomies: extroversion/introversion, sensing/intuition, thinking/feeling, and judging/perceiving. The interaction among these four preferences results in sixteen distinct personality types, each denoted by a four-letter code. Discovering that I'm an INFJ (that is, oriented toward introversion, intuition, feeling, judging) was an amazing revelation. The description nailed and validated me; among other things, INFJs are deeply emotional, empathetic, relational, and INTROVERTED.

Although it's not uncommon to be an introvert (introverts make up at least a third of the population), contemporary culture generally champions extroverted characteristics—such as being outgoing and being able to think quickly on your feet and verbalize off the top of your head—especially as a way to get ahead in life. This idealization of extroverted traits can leave us introverts feeling inadequate, excluded, or just plain weird.

Everyone falls somewhere on the extrovert/introvert continuum, and there is no one who is purely extroverted or purely introverted. I happen to be a huge introvert—I live my life inside my head, need long stretches of time alone to recharge, and prefer quiet, spacious environments. At the same time, I care very deeply about people and need the human contact that comes with love and friendship.

One of the most well-known introverted traits is an aversion to large gatherings. It's important, however, to understand that being introverted is different from being shy or antisocial. Shyness is insecurity or fear of social embarrassment, and the word "antisocial" describes someone who has hostile or harmful feelings toward society. Introversion is a preference that has to do with where you direct your energy (inward), how you recharge (usually often and by being alone), and what level of outside stimulation you're comfortable with (less is more). It's

The manual weighs more than the kid. I'm NOT delivering BOTH.
Introvert

not a weakness to overcome or something to be cured. It's just how some of us are designed.

And it's great to be an introvert! There are so many wonderful qualities that come with having this particular preference. For instance, we introverts are wired to focus and concentrate well, and we tend to process things before we speak or act. We're observant and insightful, often expressing ourselves better in writing than in speech. Because we're seriously private, introverts may be difficult to get to know, but once we warm up to someone, we make good listeners and trustworthy confidants. We prefer depth to breadth and are fiercely independent.

This book began when I found myself in a creative dry spell and needed a different medium to explore. At the same time, I found myself reflecting on how difficult life was for me growing up as an introvert and, in particular, an INFJ. Unfortunately, I didn't come with a manual. From this confluence of frustration and reflection, I invented the online personality INFJoe and began drawing and posting cartoons on the Internet. The response was amazing! To this day, I hear from people all over the world who identify with my introverted thoughts and experiences. One person wrote, "I'm so happy to find out I'm not the only one. I scored as high as possible for 'introverts.' I always felt so different and wanted to change. Now I accept it's who I am, but it makes me so happy to know there are others like me."

Navigating this extroverted world as an introvert can be tough and confusing. We're often misunderstood and left feeling unappreciated and exhausted. Sometimes we don't even understand ourselves and wish we were different. With this book, I would like to celebrate and encourage all the introverts out there. Although you prefer solitude much of the time, you're not alone; we introverts are *alone together*. If you've ever felt odd or out of place, I hope that this book will help guide you to a better understanding of yourself and that you'll feel validated and better equipped to face this extroverted world.

—Aaron Caycedo-Kimura

Know Thyself

Are you an introvert? Do you understand what that means? People are complex; no two are exactly alike. In addition to having different talents, aptitudes, physical abilities, and experiences, we fall on different points of the extrovert/introvert continuum. There are different degrees of introversion, and sometimes even introverts can have extroverted moments. But because contemporary culture idealizes extroverted traits, we introverts—especially those of us who fall on the far introverted end of the spectrum—may feel that there's something wrong with us. Some may not even understand or like themselves and may deny their natural preferences. We introverts need to understand, accept, and appreciate ourselves and how we are naturally wired. We're not weird or alien, just designed in a particular way.

Although it's possible to be all three, being introverted is not the same thing as being shy or antisocial. It's important to make the distinction. So, what makes an introvert an introvert? One primary characteristic of introversion is the preference for directing our attention inward—there's a lot going on in there!

Because we prefer to focus on the inner world, introverts are generally quiet people. That doesn't necessarily mean we're not engaged with what's going on or that we have no opinions or that we're stuck-up. We just prefer to listen and observe. We also think and process before we speak. That is, if we feel we have something worth saying.

Why are you introverts so quiet?
WHAT?!
Being "piano" is our "forte."
Google it.

Another defining characteristic of introversion is the frequent need for time alone in order to adequately recharge our batteries. Because we naturally direct our energy inward, living life in an extroverted world with all its demands can be exhausting. We need to purposefully set aside alone time and not feel guilty about it. It's a necessity.

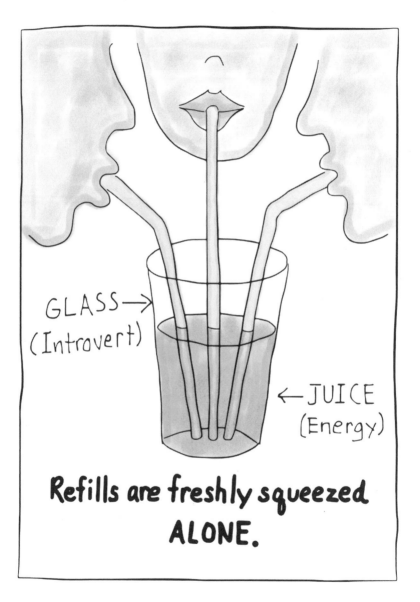

Yet another primary trait of introverts is the preference for smaller amounts of outside stimulation. We're comfortable with solitude and gravitate toward quiet environments. These are places where we do our finest work, come up with our best ideas, and dream our wildest dreams.

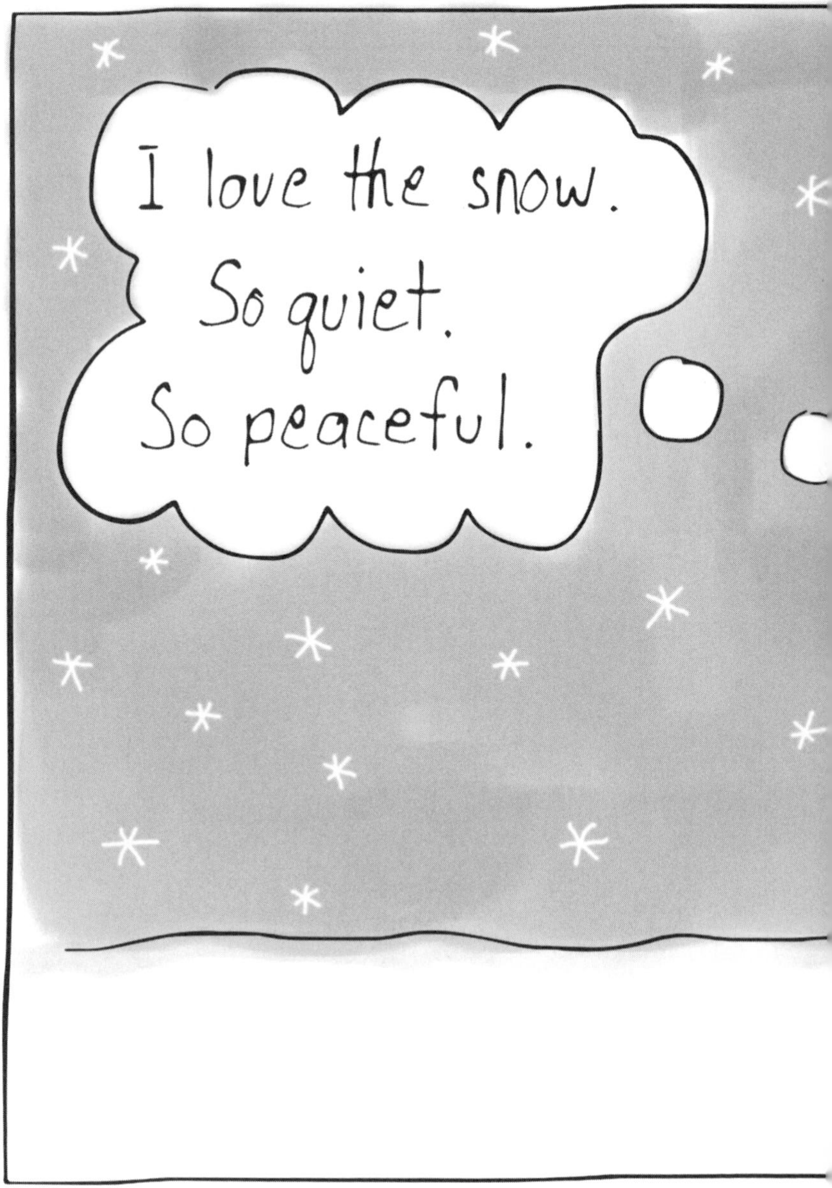
I love the snow.
So quiet.
So peaceful.

Buried in Thought

#IntrovertProblems

Do you ever feel that life is just too exhausting and over-whelming? You're not alone. On social media platforms like Twitter and Facebook, #IntrovertProblems is a popular hashtag marking the difficulties we face in leading an introverted life. It's not easy being an introvert in an overstimulating, extroverted world, having to direct massive amounts of energy outward when our preference is to direct our energy inward. On some days, just going out to the grocery store after work can seem like an impossible task, especially when all we want to do is run home and slam the door shut. On the flip side, if we stay in our heads for too long without a little outside stimulation, we can get caught in some pretty depressing introspection.

Along with dreaming and creating in our heads, we're also prone to sifting through the junk over and over. Sometimes this sifting is just so hard to turn off, and if you're losing much-needed sleep because of it, the junk only seems worse. Every once in a while, it's important to step outside our heads.

Sometimes it's not depressing introspection that's the problem. We can often get lost in thought at the wrong time if we're not careful. Fortunately, introverts are good at focusing and concentrating too, so make sure you're mentally in the right place at the right time.

You didn't hear a word I said!
What? Oh. On the contrary. I heard the word "divorce," which rhymes with "force." And that got me thinking about *Star Wars* and how cool it would be if Luke's light saber... never mind.

Being out in public is often challenging. There's really no way to completely avoid noise, people, and whatever other outside stimulation that can drain us so rapidly. If you find yourself on overload during the day, try to find a quiet corner somewhere to regain sanity.

Because introverts tend to be private, to process things more slowly, and to dislike small talk (we prefer deep, meaningful conversations), there's a certain awkwardness that can follow us. Only when we get to know someone well will that awkwardness subside. Sometimes.

Ugh. Who's comin' down the street? Should I say "hi" or is that too weird? Ugh. Too late to change sides of the street. Hey, he's got a dog! Focus on the dog!

Awkward Walk

Some Get It . . .

So, how do we cope with this extroverted world? First and foremost, we introverts need to understand, accept, and appreciate ourselves. In addition, it's helpful to have people in our lives who "get it," folks who understand the ins and outs of introversion. I was very fortunate to have had parents who were huge introverts like me. They didn't pressure me to be more outgoing but rather encouraged me to spend my time doing homework and practicing for my music lessons. Presently, most of my close friends are also introverts, and that's probably not by accident. In addition, I happen to have a few extroverts in my extended family who understand introversion and protect me at large family gatherings, making sure I have a quiet corner where people don't crowd me. If you don't have any other introverts (or sympathetic extroverts) in your life, seek them out for mutual encouragement. A third to one-half of the population is introverted, so although we may be hard to find, we're everywhere.

I want to be a writer when I grow up.
Cool. I want to be a librarian.
Cool.
AND a writer.

There's nothing like having a good friend who's introverted too. There are no unwarranted explanations or awkward excuses needed. They understand because they do the same introverted things that you do.

It's a rare gift to have extroverts in your life who get it. Cherish them! Because they're at home in stimulating environments, like fish in water, they're good at pushing you to the surface when you feel as if you're drowning.

OK, folks. Take it easy. Two steps back. I'm an extroverted member of Adopt an Introvert, and you're all crowding my boy here.

Just coming across someone in our day who gets it, whether we know them well or not, is encouraging. It reminds us that we're not alone. Keep an eye out for these people. You'll be surprised at how many you find.

Because of our nature, it may take too much energy to connect with another introvert you don't know. If you don't have enough people in your real life who get it, social media is a great place to connect with other introverts.

Hey, going out with all of us tonight?
No, thanks. Need some introvert alone time.
With my 423 Facebook and Twitter friends.

Wow, it's all over the Internet. I guess introversion is the new extroversion.

Word of warning: when people get it, things may not always work in our favor, such as when parents know how to dole out appropriate punishment or when people who love being around us just can't seem to get enough of us.

... and Some Don't

Let's face it—some folks just don't get it, and as a result, we introverts are quite often misunderstood. This is probably the most frustrating of all #IntrovertProblems. At one time or another, we may have felt the sting of someone saying, "What's wrong with you?" or "Why are you so quiet?" or "Why can't you be more outgoing?" We may have heard these things from well-meaning (and not-so-well-meaning) friends, family members, teachers, or co-workers. It's a good idea to try to educate people about extroversion and introversion, but there will always be folks who don't understand even when we try to explain ourselves.

Sorry, Sue. John's tired and wants to stay in tonight. Says he needs to recharge. Some kind of "introvert" thing. What? You'll bring the party HERE?! GREAT!!

There's no use in trying to turn us into something we're not. It would be like expecting an orange tree to produce apples just because you prefer apples. I spent many years trying to be extroverted, and all that got me was frustration, exhaustion, and an inauthentic self that I presented to the world.

I'm determined to get you out of your shell. I think you'd be happier like us.

You comin' to the party tonight?
No. Thanks. We have a nice quiet evening planned with takeout, a movie, and a bottle of wine.
OK, but remember, you GOT to have fun sometimes.
Um, yeah.

An introvert's kind of fun is not necessarily an extrovert's kind of fun. We're wired for less outside stimulation than they are, so what's relaxing and enjoyable for us may be boring for them. They may never understand, so just be yourself.

It's not you. It's me.
Why don't you want to be with me? I'm the life of the party!
OK, it IS you.

You know, Pete, you gotta get out more. Don't you wanna be more popular? You're dull and boring because your life is dull and boring.

Introverts generally hate being the center of attention, or worse, being scrutinized. Quiet and soft-spoken, we're not waiting to be thrust into the spotlight. Sometimes it's unavoidable. At other times, it's OK to politely excuse yourself and walk away.

What's different about you? New hairdo? No. New eye shadow? No. Teeth whitening? No, that's not it. Hey, Steve-o, come over here and help me figure this out.
Go. A-way.

To an introvert, phone calls can be intrusive. They also lack important visual cues. Face-to-face silences can be awkward, but dead air during a phone conversation is unbearable. If it's a close friend, a prearranged business call, or an acquaintance who lives far away, we'll take the call, but we prefer texting or emailing. It's a good idea to let people know your preferred method of communication.

Talking on the
phone is painful,

Surviving Large Groups

I t's fairly well-known that introverts have a general aversion to large groups of people. This is not to say we're incapable of attending and even enjoying, to a degree, large social events. Even extreme introverts can find meaningful conversations or experiences within large groups of people. Usually, the meaningful interaction is with another introvert. However, it's safe to say that even with a gathering of good friends, the outside overstimulation will take its toll. We get drained in overstimulating environments, which can include lots of people, loud noises or music, bright lights, and constant movement. Our energy can deplete just by being in a crowd without even talking to anyone. It's our Kryptonite.

C'mon. Let's go to the party.
I have to finish my book.
She dies in the end.
We all do. Still not going.

In addition to the outside overstimulation of large groups, there's also all that stuff that goes on in our heads that takes its toll. We don't just physically go to a party, concert, or game. It's an entire mental and emotional event.

For the introvert, socializing isn't just about the social event itself. It's also about the anticipation before and the unwinding after.

Why do I have to go to the party? I've played it all out in my head, and I'm exhausted!

It's important to point out that introverts are social beings like everyone else. We don't hate people. We just prefer to socialize differently from extroverts. We like one-on-one interactions (or small get-togethers of three or four) because they give us the opportunity to have private, in-depth conversations. They allow us to give our undivided attention and to have a greater chance of being heard when we have something to say. In a one-on-one situation, introverts can be quite talkative, whereas in larger groups we tend to clam up.

So I'll see you at seven. Can't wait for some quiet catch-up time with you. It's been so long.
Oh, by the way, I invited Sue, Jen, Stevie, and Rhonda to come too. Jesse and Vicki said "maybe." It'll be great!

So, how do we survive large groups? The first solution, of course, is avoiding the crowd. But if you can't, there are ways to reduce the inevitable impact. Make sure you get time alone to recharge before and after the event. While at the event, you can zero in on another introvert to hang out with, or you can "hide out" by helping in the kitchen or stepping outside for some fresh air.

What are you doing this weekend?
Nothing.
Wanna come over?
Thank you, but no. Nothing is something.

Introvert Recon
North, east, and south exits. Restrooms in lobby outside east exit. Food and drink tables at west wall. Another introvert next to the ficus at 2 o'clock.
WELCOME 25TH REUNION

One thing about large groups is that there's bound to be a lot of small talk going on. Although we dislike small talk, keep in mind that it can sometimes lead to a more in-depth conversation. I find that if you ask the right questions concerning what people are interested in or passionate about, they open up and often share their true selves. If the conversation doesn't get past small talk, it's OK to move on.

The result of spending time in a large group is feeling "peopled out," and everyone experiences this differently. Sometimes I find myself feeling out of sorts and don't know why until I realize that I've recently been around a lot of people. I might have even had a good time, but there's always fallout, just the same. The remedy is always alone time to recharge.

Navigating the Workplace

Here we go. Where do I even start? What's with the open floor plans? If we're not going to get offices, at least give us cubicles. And even though we're great listeners, please don't come talk to us every ten minutes. We actually have work to do. I think we introverts can do without meetings, unless they are to the point and not an excuse for more socializing. Likewise, teamwork should be efficient, with everyone doing his or her part. Drinks after work? After spending all day with our co-workers in a fluorescent-lit box, we'd like to go home. It's not an easy thing for an introvert to spend eight hours a day, five days a week (sometimes more), with continual interaction in a closed environment.

Introverts go to work primarily for one thing: to work. We're not really there to socialize, although working with a good group of people is rewarding. Introvert work philosophy can be summed up like this: give me a strong shovel, show me where to dig, then leave me alone. But to be a good employee, it's important to develop good interpersonal skills while keeping your work ethic intact.

Know when you have to grin and bear it and when you can give yourself a break. There's such a thing as going above and beyond in doing your job, but there's also living to fight another day. Make sure you do your job well while avoiding burnout.

How does Joe get into his cubicle? There's even a top on this thing.
Is he even in there?
Email Me.

Introverts may find themselves in work situations that push them way out of their comfort zones. The key to facing many of these challenges is preparation. If you have a scheduled meeting with an open discussion, find out ahead of time what the discussion topics are. If you're making a big presentation, try to give yourself enough time to rehearse. For other situations, such as meeting new clients for the first time, try to anticipate likely scenarios and prepare accordingly.

Let's face it—because the workplace is made up of other people, there's always a certain amount of socializing that needs to be done in and around the office. Sometimes we just have to rise to the occasion and put our best extroverted foot forward. Know when you can handle it and when you can't, and keep in mind that others may genuinely want your company.

Hey, everyone! Cindy's going with us to Skip's for drinks after work today! Can you believe it?!. Who would've thunk it in a million years!!
Forget it.

Getting Through the
Holidays and Other
Celebrations

Do you look forward to holidays and birthdays? Do you like the festivities, or do you dread them? Special days and events offer a time of reflection, which we introverts love to do. They prompt us to think about such things as what we're thankful for, how we can be more giving, what it means to be patriotic, or how our particular spiritual beliefs affect our lives. However, these are also times of family gatherings, office parties, and large crowded events that introverts don't love so much. These events can easily become an added stress in an already challenging existence.

I know you didn't want me to throw you a birthday party, but my friends and I had a great time. Hope you did too.

If you're able, keep holidays and other celebrations intimate. Share them with a special someone or with the few people closest to you. Make it a tradition, and along with it, make some memories that you can look back on with great fondness.

Here, Honey. A 32-pack of Valentine's Day cards. That's enough for your entire class.
But I only want 3.

Focus on what the occasion means to you personally, and take some time to reflect. Even if large groups are in your plans, the holiday doesn't have to totally be about the dreaded family get-together or office party. You can read a book related to the holiday, do some arts and crafts, or write a poem, story, or essay.

OK, everyone! Get in the car. We're going to the Independence Day parade!
This year I'm declaring my independence and staying home.
I said, "Get in the car."

When there's no avoiding a larger crowd, join in the celebration with abandon. Go to that party. Go to that family get-together. Take small breaks in the midst of them, and if possible, leave early. Don't forget to set aside lots of alone time afterwards. You'll need it!

I mean, you already have a kids' table right? Why not have an introverts' table? Maybe slip it right into the den. It doesn't even have to be an actual table.

What I look like after the holidays.

What I feel like.

Introvert Bliss

When we understand, accept, and appreciate our introversion, we become more at peace with ourselves. We learn how to tap into our strengths and protect our vulnerabilities. We spend time doing the things we love to do in the way we love to do them, without guilt or embarrassment. We can revel in what we do best: ponder the deeper things of life, cultivate ideas, enjoy our solitude, and, at other times, enjoy being alone together with someone close to us. It's great to be an introvert, and going with the flow of our natural preference makes all the difference in the world.

The introverted mind is a pretty inspiring place to be. A lot goes on in there that people don't know about. It's a private place, a retreat, a laboratory, a library, a maze for us to get lost in.

Get that alone time to recharge, and enjoy it. I can't stress that enough. Set your boundaries. It's for the good of everyone in your immediate life. It allows you to give yourself and those around you your very best.

Any plans for this weekend?
Triathlon.
Wow. Swim, cycle, run?
No. Book, bath, nap.

Find your happy place, whether it's doing what you love to do alone or with a special someone. Be good to yourself. Be true to yourself.

I thought you introverts preferred peace and quiet.
My own noise doesn't count.

Wow, it's so quiet and peaceful. So introverted. Let's go for a walk.

With special thanks to Emily Haynes of
BluePen Agency, Lauren Appleton and
Jeanette Shaw of TarcherPerigee,
Jenn Granneman of *Introvert, Dear*, and
all the online readers of INFJoe Cartoons.

Ugh. Make it quick. I hate taking pictures. C'mon. People are starting to watch.

About the Author

INFJoe is the nom de cartoon of artist Aaron Caycedo-Kimura. Born and raised in Santa Rosa, California, Aaron drummed his way to The Juilliard School in New York City via the San Francisco Conservatory of Music. During postgraduate soul-searching, he realized that he had always been more visually oriented than aurally oriented. Turning to visual art, he picked up computer graphics to pay the bills and a paintbrush to feed his soul. From the subways and cramped apartments of New York City, Aaron and his wife, Luisa, relocated to the suburbs of Fairfield County, Connecticut, where he studied at the Silvermine School of Art in New Canaan. In 2012, Aaron and Luisa moved to Boston, where INFJoe was conceived and Luisa earned an MFA in poetry at Boston University. Now back in Connecticut, they plan to finally settle down and birth as much art as possible.